Social Media Management Mastery

Build a Lucrative Business in the Digital World

Table of Contents

1. Introduction 1

2. Understanding the Power of Social Media 2

   2.1. The Demographics of Social Media 2

   2.2. The Mechanics of Content Sharing 3

   2.3. Dealing with the Pace of Social Media 3

   2.4. The Power of Social Listening 3

   2.5. Influencer Marketing and Collaboration 4

   2.6. The Ins and Outs of Analytics 4

   2.7. Cultivating a Brand Identity on Social Media 5

   2.8. The Potential of Paid Advertising 5

3. The Art of Crafting Engaging Content 6

   3.1. The Essence of Engaging Content 6

   3.2. The Building Blocks of Engagement 7

   3.3. Unpacking the Interest of Your Audience 7

   3.4. Riding the Wave of Relevance 8

   3.5. Unleashing the Power of Creativity 8

   3.6. Harnessing Authenticity 8

   3.7. Consistent Delivery 9

4. Hidden Secrets of Social Media Platforms 10

   4.1. From Algorithms to Activations: Understanding Platform
Mechanisms 10

   4.2. A World Beyond Likes 10

   4.3. UX/UI: Crafting the Digital Experience 11

   4.4. Ephemeral Content: Harnessing the Temporal 11

   4.5. Data Reigns Supreme 11

   4.6. Privacy and Authenticity: Winning in the Age of
Transparency 11

   4.7. From Social Networks to Marketplaces 12

4.8. Social Media Advertising: Making Your Brand Shine 12

4.9. Collaboration and Influencer Marketing 12

4.10. Riding the Viral Wave 13

4.11. Crisis Management on Social Platforms 13

5. The Role of Analytics in Social Media Management 14

5.1. Understanding Social Media Analytics 14

5.2. Importance of setting KPIs 15

5.3. Decoding Key Social Media Metrics 15

5.4. Leveraging Social Media Data for Brand Positioning 16

5.5. A/B Testing and Social Media Analytics 16

5.6. The Future of Social Media Analytics 16

6. Designing a Winning Social Media Strategy 18

6.1. Define Business and Social Media Goals 18

6.2. Know your Audience 19

6.3. Choosing the Right Social Media Platforms 19

6.4. Creating a Content Strategy 19

6.5. Consistent Branding 20

6.6. Regular Engagement 20

6.7. Social Media Analytics 20

6.8. Social Media Scheduling 20

6.9. Crisis Management Plan 21

7. The Socio-Psychological Cornerstones of User Engagement 22

7.1. Emotional Connectivity in Digital Spaces 22

7.2. Profiling and Segmentation for Tailored Interaction 22

7.3. Authenticity and Transparency: Creating Trust 23

7.4. Cultivating a Unique Voice and Persona 24

7.5. Content Strategies for Active Participation and
Collaboration 24

7.6. Reactionary Marketing: Quick Adaptability 25

8. Conquering Crisis: Damage Control in Digital Spaces 26

8.1. When Crises Emerge 26

8.2. The Art of Crisis Identification 26

8.3. Crafting a Response Plan 27

8.4. Devising a Communication Strategy 27

8.5. Crisis Resolution and Learning from Mistakes 28

9. Monetizing Your Social Media Presence 29

9.1. Establishing a Strong Brand Identity 29

9.2. Creating Engaging Content 30

9.3. Diversifying Revenue Streams 30

9.4. Harnessing the Power of Analytics 31

9.5. Building Community and Fostering Engagement 32

10. Effective Use of Influencer Marketing 33

10.1. Understanding Influencer Marketing 33

10.2. Crafting an Effective Influencer Strategy 33

10.3. Measuring Success in Influencer Marketing 34

10.4. Avoiding Common Influencer Marketing Pitfalls 34

10.5. Building Long-Term Relationships 35

11. Staying Ahead: Anticipating Digital Communication Trends . . . 36

11.1. Understanding the Importance of Anticipating Trends 36

11.2. Analyzing Market Behavior 36

11.3. Utilizing Technology in Trend Forecasting 37

11.4. Social Listening for Digital Communication Trends 37

11.5. Evaluating and Adapting 38

11.6. Experimental Attitudes and Testing New Platforms 38

11.7. Looking Into Future Trends 38

Chapter 1. Introduction

Welcome to a breathtaking new era of entrepreneurship in the lively realm of digital communications! This Special Report, "Social Media Management Mastery: Build a Lucrative Business in the Digital World," serves as your trusted guide into this enchanting landscape. No stodgy tech jargon here; instead, we distill the essence of success for manageable, relatable concepts ripe for the taking. Sure, there are technical aspects, but that's not our prime focus - the real gem here is the potential for prosperity. By harnessing the virility of social media, learning to engage effectively within its landscapes, and understanding how to ride its ever-moving currents, the world of digital entrepreneurship opens up before you. So join us as we delve deep into understanding the heart of modern business, and let us inspire and motivate you to take a leap into the vibrant world of social media management that may very well lead you towards building a lucrative business of your own!

Chapter 2. Understanding the Power of Social Media

The digital revolution has bestowed us with a tool that possesses unparalleled power – Social Media. It's more than just a platform to showcase your daily life or connect with your old pals. The individuals and businesses that have decoded its true potential, weaved their magic around it, and harnessed its strength, have emerged as frontrunners in their respective fields.

2.1. The Demographics of Social Media

Understanding demographics is paramount to the usage of social media effectively. The existing user base and the prospects of particular platforms provide the insights required to cultivate the content and the strategic approach suitable for a specific audience.

Facebook is the unrivaled king when it comes to widespread usage. Grandmothers, school teachers, college students - you'll find every age group scrolling through their feed. Instagram, bought by Facebook in 2012, has a slightly younger audience, favoring photo and video content. Twitter is a great platform for real-time communication, while LinkedIn serves as a professional network.

How age, gender, occupation, interests, and behavior characterize the user base of these platforms is the key to formulate a successful social media strategy. Each platform serves a different purpose and supports distinctive styles of content, hence it requires a tailored strategy.

2.2. The Mechanics of Content Sharing

The next piece of this puzzle is understanding how people share content. Different platforms use different algorithms to decide what content to show a user. Understanding this can exponentially increase the reach of your content.

Knowing how likes, shares, comments, and even views affect your content's visibility can provide an upper hand when engaging with your audience. Each interaction by a user boosts the visibility of the content, amplifying its reach. This underlying mechanism fuels the concept of virality, and knowing how to navigate this can catapult one's online presence.

2.3. Dealing with the Pace of Social Media

Social media doesn't operate on a 9-to-5 schedule. It's a 24/7 world that's constantly shifting and evolving. Keeping up with its pace can be challenging, but understanding this fast-paced environment is essential.

Daily trends, news, memes come and go at lightning speed. To keep your audience engaged, timely participation in these trending topics can prove beneficial. Embracing current happenings and weaving them into your narratives can enhance your connection with the audience.

2.4. The Power of Social Listening

If content is the king, then social listening is the queen. It shapes understanding of what your audience is saying about you and your industry. Monitoring keywords, hashtags, and conversations around your brand can provide valuable customer insights, which can refine your marketing strategies. This is the essence of social listening – turning cyber noise into actionable insights.

2.5. Influencer Marketing and Collaboration

The advent of social media influencers has revolutionized digital marketing. They can enhance brand awareness, drive audience engagement, and promote products or services with authenticity.

Partnerships or collaborations with influencers relevant to your industry can create a win-win situation. Their endorsements can further affirm your brand's credibility and broaden your reach. Figuring out these collaboration opportunities can be a game-changer.

2.6. The Ins and Outs of Analytics

Data is the lifeblood of social media marketing. Relying on gut feelings is not enough when billions of likes, shares, comments, and views generate valuable data trails. This information can illuminate what works and what doesn't, helping mold effective social media campaigns.

Most social media platforms provide built-in analytics tools. Mastering these can help steer your strategy in the right direction, ensuring that your efforts culminate into maximum benefits.

2.7. Cultivating a Brand Identity on Social Media

Your profiles on social platforms form the first impression of your brand for many users. Creating a consistent and authentic brand identity across all affiliated social media accounts is a necessity. Consistency in color themes, tonality, mission, and vision enhances brand recognition, resulting in better audience engagement.

2.8. The Potential of Paid Advertising

Organically growing your social media reach is a long-term game. For quicker results, paid advertising comes into play. An adept understanding of targeting demographics, interests, and behaviors can lead to effective ad campaigns. Even with small budgets, your content can reach a vast audience, provided you understand your audience well.

It's clear now that the power of social media in the realm of digital entrepreneurship cannot be underestimated. By understanding its dynamics, not only can you engage effectively but also ride its ever-moving currents towards building a lucrative business in the digital world. This chapter has, by no means, covered everything. Social media is a vast and ever-evolving concept. The ability to remain open-minded, adapt to changing trends, and constantly learn is the aptitude you will require to secure lucrative prospects in this digital age. Every twist and turn in this journey has something to teach you, so anticipate the unexpected, embrace the changes, and most importantly - keep learning.

Chapter 3. The Art of Crafting Engaging Content

Just as blood pumps from the heart, spreading vitality throughout the body, so does content drive the life force of social media, carrying the core essence of your message and brand. Indeed, the crafting of engaging content in the aspirational landscape of the digital world is an art, demanding creativity alongside a deep understanding of audience sentiment, plus an innate sense for timing, relevance, and the rapidly evolving trends of social media.

3.1. The Essence of Engaging Content

From multinational corporations holding billions under their command to a slew of budding entrepreneurs presenting their unique products and services before the world, everyone is vying for attention in the digital sphere. That's where the artistry of crafting engaging content comes in. But what is engaging content?

Indeed, an elusive question. Does it lie in the quirkiness of a caption, the creativity of a video, or the offbeat meme you shared? Yes, it could be any of these. Yet, remember, what engages one does not necessarily engage all. And here lies the crux - to understand and deliver what creates a connection with your specific audience. Engaging content captures attention, preserving precious moments in the viewers' minds, encouraging their interaction, and ultimately, forging a deeper connection with your brand.

3.2. The Building Blocks of Engagement

To create engaging content, you need a foundation with solid blocks. In a broad sense, these blocks can be categorized into:

1. Knowing Your Audience: Craft content based on need, interest, preference, and the demographics of your target audience.

2. Relevance: Understand the ongoing themes, trends, and events affecting your audience, and align your content accordingly.

3. Creativity: Innovate and experiment with various formats- texts, images, videos, infographics, memes, etc.

4. Authenticity: Be true to your brand. Authenticity creates trust, a vital ingredient for engagement.

5. Consistency: Maintain a steady stream of content to keep your audience engaged and looking forward to more.

3.3. Unpacking the Interest of Your Audience

Every brand consists of a unique mix of diverse individuals, each with their specific preferences and expectations. To craft content that strikes a chord, your first step is to understand the people within your audience.

Demographic data provides a good starting point - age, gender, location, education, and occupation. But to truly create compelling content, delve further. Understand their psychographics – their values, attitudes, interests, lifestyle, and personality traits. Use polls, questionnaires, and social media analytics tools to gather this information. Seek to comprehend their challenges, what solutions they need, and importantly, how they consume content.

3.4. Riding the Wave of Relevance

Engaging content is timely and fluid, morphing with the evolving trends and scenarios within society and the lives of your audience. Herein, there's space to draw parallels between your brand offerings and the ongoing themes, headlines, holidays, and events.

However, it's crucial to maintain sensitivity while trying to be relevant. Remember, engagement thrives in respect and understanding. Also, overuse of trends for the sake of being trendy can sometimes lead to disconnect. Therefore, always ensure relevance aligns with your brand and audience.

3.5. Unleashing the Power of Creativity

Creativity infuses life into your content. In an online world peppered with a barrage of images, videos, and text, creativity differentiates and uplifts your content. Let your creativity flow through storytelling, humor, innovative formats, eye-catching visuals, or by simply presenting mundane facts in an interesting way. Remember to balance creativity with relevance and understanding of your audience.

3.6. Harnessing Authenticity

Gone are days of glossy advertisements promising dreamy utopias. Today's digital audience seeks authenticity. They appreciate transparent, real, and relatable content. Embrace your brand's uniqueness, share your journey, your successes, and also your failures. Authenticity humanizes your brand, paving the way for engagement based on trust and relationship.

3.7. Consistent Delivery

Lastly, engagement is not a one-time event but a sustained effort. Amid the transience of digital content, maintaining consistency is key. Consistency isn't just about frequency; it's also about voice, theme, and quality. A consistent content strategy fosters anticipation for your next piece, incubates brand loyalty, and fosters a deeper connection.

Remember, the art of crafting engaging content is an ongoing process of learning, experimenting, and adapting. With time, you'll discover what delights, intrigues, and call your audience to engage. It's a woven tapestry of science, art, and human understanding, forever changing and forever magical!

Chapter 4. Hidden Secrets of Social Media Platforms

Just as a magician never reveals his tricks, social media platforms also contain many features and mechanisms that, while not quite secrets, are often overlooked by their users. By unraveling these so-called 'secrets', one can gain a profound understanding and consequently, have a significant advantage in navigating and mastering these platforms.

4.1. From Algorithms to Activations: Understanding Platform Mechanisms

When your post goes live, its fate lies in the hands of the platform's algorithm. Be it Instagram's image recognition or Twitter's trend tracking, understanding these mechanisms is critical. Explore the algorithm's stakeholders, including users, the items they share, and the intricate relations between them. Comprehend how factors such as timing, location, and user interactions influence post visibility. Moreover, approach activation methods—email notifications, push alerts, and more—strategically to connect with users without overwhelming them.

4.2. A World Beyond Likes

A "Like" isn't just a simple appreciation. Instead, it involves psychological nuances. It can serve as a social tool, broadcasting views, affirming identities, or maintaining relationships. Furthermore, other user reactions—comments, shares, saves—carry their meanings. Identifying these behavioral patterns can help tailor content strategies.

4.3. UX/UI: Crafting the Digital Experience

User experience (UX) and user interface (UI) are intertwined in holding the users captive within a platform. Studying UI, pay attention to design elements governing user navigation and decision-making. Meanwhile, a smooth UX is vital for user retention and involves factors like load speeds and app crashes. Understanding UX/UI can optimize your posts' presentation and deliverability.

4.4. Ephemeral Content: Harnessing the Temporal

Temporary posts, like Instagram stories and Snapchat snaps, bring a unique allure. They tap into the fear of missing out (FOMO) effect, driving user engagement upwards. Craft ephemeral content strategies to hold the audience's swift attention.

4.5. Data Reigns Supreme

Pay attention to the numerous data points generated. These could range from post engagements, impressions, and followers' demographics to more nuanced data like user-comment sentiment. Moreover, understand how various A/B testing strategies work, driving intelligent strategy improvement.

4.6. Privacy and Authenticity: Winning in the Age of Transparency

Anticipate users' concerns about privacy and manipulation. Navigate the fine line between effective targeting and intrusion. Simultaneously, foster authenticity, often lauded as a vital part of brand voice. Brands seen as relatable and honest often enjoy more user trust and loyalty, which eventually translates into engagement and revenue.

4.7. From Social Networks to Marketplaces

Explore the capabilities of platforms as marketplaces. Facebook Marketplace, Instagram Shopping are all opportunities to tap into e-commerce. Understand how consumers use these features and how you can leverage them to boost conversions and sales.

4.8. Social Media Advertising: Making Your Brand Shine

Understand how sponsored content works. Know the formats, guidelines, and best practices of placing sponsored content for maximum impact. You'll also need to know how to decode advertisement performance metrics to understand what's working for your brand and what's not.

4.9. Collaboration and Influencer Marketing

Identify and engage industry influencers or bloggers for partnerships. Understand how these collaborations work, how compensation varies, and what kind of results you can expect. Develop a guideline for influencer identification, content creation, and campaign analysis.

4.10. Riding the Viral Wave

Decipher what makes a post go viral. From a perfectly timed tweet to a relatable meme, viral content can significantly boost brand visibility and engagement. Understand the elements of viral content and strategies for creating your viral campaign.

4.11. Crisis Management on Social Platforms

Lastly, understand the mitigation strategies for a social media crisis. Be it a disgruntled customer or a public relations nightmare, knowing how to handle these situations effectively is a significant part of social media management.

As we've explored, there's so much more to social media than meets the eye. By truly understanding the mechanics, capabilities, and limitations of these platforms, we can build strategies that not only stay on the pulse of digital trends but reshape them. After all, in the transformative realm of digital communications, being a master rather than a novice can make all the difference.

Chapter 5. The Role of Analytics in Social Media Management

In the vibrant world of social media management, understanding and harnessing the power of analytics is akin to possessing a compass in uncharted territory. Being capable of decoding data can give your business the advantage it needs to cut through the noise and reach the right audience at the right time with the right content.

5.1. Understanding Social Media Analytics

Social media is a constant, cascading stream of interactions and engagement. Every day, millions of users post, like, share, and comment, thereby creating an enormous amount of data. Social media analytics shines a discerning light on this colossal collection of information, extracting patterns, identifying trends, and revealing clear paths to optimized social media strategies. Put simply, social media analytics allows businesses to convert raw data into actionable insight.

Just like listening in on millions of conversations to find out what's relevant for your business, social media analytics gives you a kind of "social listening" ability, where you can tune in to what is being said about your brand, your competitors, and your industry as a whole. Metrics like engagement rate, reach, impressions, and sentiment analysis provide you with insights into your social media performance and audience behavior.

5.2. Importance of setting KPIs

Before diving into the analysis of data, it is fundamental to set clear Key Performance Indicators (KPIs). These parameters will vary depending on your strategic objectives, whether they include boosting brand awareness, driving sales, improving customer service, or any other unique goals of your business.

KPIs translate your business objectives into measurable metrics, creating a bridge between strategy and execution. For instance, if your objective is to increase brand awareness through social media, your KPIs can include metrics like follower growth rate, post reach, impressions, and brand mentions.

5.3. Decoding Key Social Media Metrics

Now that we've established why insights from social media analytics are crucial and the importance of setting KPIs aligned to your business goals, it's time to engage with four fundamental analytic metrics every social media manager should master.

1. Reach: This refers to the number of unique viewers who see your social media post. Not to be confused with impressions, which counts the total number of times your content is displayed, regardless if it was clicked or not.

2. Engagement: This metric demonstrates how your audience interacts with your content. It includes likes, shares, replies, comments, mentions, clicks, and even video views.

3. Conversion rate: Represents how many positive actions (such as a purchase or a signup) resulted from your social media activity. This metric directly correlates to ROI (Return on Investment) and is invaluable when demonstrating the efficacy of social media efforts in monetary terms.

4. Customer sentiment: Although harder to quantify, understanding customer sentiment through analyzing comments and interactions can help brands understand how their content is received, and how brand perception might be shifting.

5.4. Leveraging Social Media Data for Brand Positioning

Understanding these metrics is the first step. The real magic happens when you apply this knowledge for decision-making purposes. Businesses can use this data-driven insights to reposition their brands, understand trending conversations within their industry, develop targeted campaigns, and ultimately differentiate themselves from the competition.

5.5. A/B Testing and Social Media Analytics

To further refine your social media strategies, continuous testing and adaptation are indispensable. One popular form of experimentation is A/B testing, where you alter one variable at a time (such as headline, image, or call to action) between two pieces of content to see which performs better. Social media analytics offers the tools to track the effectiveness of these tests, informing your ongoing strategy.

5.6. The Future of Social Media Analytics

As we move forward in the digital era, social media analytics will continue to evolve. We already see the rise of AI and machine learning in analytics, offering predictive patterns and automating complex analysis. With the pace of technology, who knows what the landscape will look like in the near future?

Whether you're a novice entrepreneur or a seasoned business vet, a grasp of social media analytics is key to charting a profitable course in the dazzling world of digital communications. By arming yourself with knowledge of key metrics and understanding how to apply these insights, you're well on your way to mastering the art of analytics in social media management.

Chapter 6. Designing a Winning Social Media Strategy

Understanding your business and target audience is your initial step in sparking the life of your social media strategy. Imagine attempting to hit a target blindfolded; that's what it's like trying to cultivate a successful social media plan without knowing your business objectives and audience. Let's define the path ahead meticulously.

6.1. Define Business and Social Media Goals

Start by aligning your business goals with your social media objectives. What would you like to achieve through your venture into social media channels?

- Is it Brand Awareness: To introduce your offering to a larger audience?

- Lead Generation: Capturing prospective customers?

- Sales: Converting those leads into active clients?

- Customer Retention: Ensuring clients remain satisfied and loyal?

- Community Engagement: Building a vibrant online network that champions your brand?

Knowing the answer helps tailor content, target the right audience, and choose the right platforms.

6.2. Know your Audience

Knowing your audience is imperative in designing your social media strategy. Consider their demographics, from age, gender, location, to employment status, interests, and preferences. You should also understand their behavior online - which platforms they frequent, their peak online hours, and the type of content they engage with.

Tools such as Google Analytics, Facebook Insights, and Instagram Insights provide these data, enabling you to tailor your content and post timing for better engagement.

6.3. Choosing the Right Social Media Platforms

Not every platform will be right for your business. Engaging on too many can spread your efforts too thin, producing subpar results. Your audience research provides some insight into where your potential clients spend their time. Where they are, you should be.

For instance, if you're targeting young adults, Instagram and TikTok might be your best bet, whilst LinkedIn may serve best for B2B services.

6.4. Creating a Content Strategy

Content is the lifeblood of social media. What you put out into the digital sphere will define your brand, engage your audience, and call them to action.

Define your content mix: Consider using a blend of informational content (blogs, guides, how-tos), entertainment content (games, quizzes, memes related to your industry), promotional content (offers, discounts, new product launch), and user-generated content (client testimonials, reviews, customer posts).

6.5. Consistent Branding

Each post represents your brand. Maintaining consistency in terms of tone, visual elements, and messaging helps customers recognise and relate to your brand.

Consider creating a brand guide that specifies the color palette, typography, imagery style, and tone of voice to be used across social media platforms.

6.6. Regular Engagement

Modern customers expect brands to speak 'with' them, not 'to' them. Ensure to engage with your audience regularly. Respond to comments, share user-generated content, and don't shy away from showcasing your brand personality.

6.7. Social Media Analytics

This section details the importance of tracking your goals, understanding metrics, and interpreting data. Social media analytics can offer a wealth of information to assess the effectiveness of your strategy.

Track Key Performance Indicators (KPIs), like follower growth rate, engagement rate, click-through rate, conversion rate, and more. Adjust your strategy based on your analytic reports to maximise performance.

6.8. Social Media Scheduling

Manually posting content on various platforms daily would be a herculean task. Tools like Hootsuite, Buffer, or Sprout Social allow you to schedule your posts for days or even weeks ahead, saving time and ensuring regularity.

6.9. Crisis Management Plan

In the age of viral posts, having a crisis management plan is crucial. Identify potential risks, draft template responses and establish a response strategy. The faster you can address an issue, the better.

Designing a winning social media strategy is a process of continual refinement. It must be flexible, but always aligning with your business's voice and values. With focus, authenticity, and a little bit of digital charm, the landscape of social media management is ripe for the taking. Seize it, and watch opportunities for customer engagement, brand growth, and financial success flourish.

Chapter 7. The Socio-Psychological Cornerstones of User Engagement

The road to effective social media management isn't just filled with learning to navigate different platforms, creating effective content, or mastering SEO. It also involves a critical understanding of foundational socio-psychological principles that highlight what draws users in, keeps them engaged, and motivates them to return.

7.1. Emotional Connectivity in Digital Spaces

For many, social media are not just about scrolling through curated feeds but rather, places of emotional resonance. Users seek content that resonates with their beliefs, attitudes, aspirations, and fears. As a social media manager, understanding the emotional landscape of your audience is key. This involves identifying the general emotional tone of your target demographic and subsequently, curating content that elicits the desired emotive responses.

But, how does one chart the emotional landscape of an audience? You do it by following the conversations, by understanding the trending topics, and by reflecting on uproarious memes. A social media manager must become a sociologist of sorts to tap into the emotionally-charged conversations that captivate their audience.

7.2. Profiling and Segmentation for Tailored Interaction

Personalization is the cornerstone of successful user engagement. To achieve this, you should start by profiling and segmenting your audience. Profiling involves collecting and analysing data related to user behavior, preferences, and interests. You can then categorize (or segment) your users based on these data, tailoring content and interactions according to their respective profiles.

Your segmentation can be demographic — based on age, gender, location, etc. It could also be psychographic, reflecting users' lifestyles, values, personalities, and interests, or behavioral, taking into account users' activities, interactions and engagement patterns with your content.

Remember, the goal of segmentation is to offer tailored experiences that incite meaningful engagement — a mass-market approach rarely works in the nuanced world of social media.

7.3. Authenticity and Transparency: Creating Trust

Nothing turns users away faster than inauthentic content. Users are increasingly savvy when it comes to the content they consume and are often quick to detect deceptive or overly promotional material. Authenticity, therefore, stands as a paramount principle in fostering user engagement.

Sharing content that genuinely reflects your brand, engaging in open and authentic dialogue with your audience, and promptly addressing concerns can cultivate a sense of trust and connectedness.

Transparency builds on the authenticity drive, as it entails openly sharing your successes, admitting your failures, and honestly addressing criticism. Social media users value emotional honesty and vulnerability, and transparency in your communication can often lead to deeper engagement from your audience.

7.4. Cultivating a Unique Voice and Persona

Having a distinctive voice is not only about standing out in the sea of digital content. It's also about consistently showcasing who you are and what you stand for, which can strengthen your brand image and create a more relatable and engaging presence for your users.

The voice and persona you cultivate should align with your audience's expectations and your brand's values, creating a seamless link between your online persona and your offline identity.

7.5. Content Strategies for Active Participation and Collaboration

To win the social media field, your approach should facilitate active user participation and collaboration. Here are a few notable strategies:

1. Creation of User-Generated Content (UGC): Encouraging users to create and share their own content not only generates engagement but can greatly enhance your credibility.

2. Hosting Collaborative Challenges and Competitions: Staging creative contests encourages user participation and fosters a sense of community.

3. Facilitating Discussions: Posting open-ended questions and hosting live Q&As are effective ways to promote engagement while offering valuable insights into your audience's thoughts, opinions, and interests.

7.6. Reactionary Marketing: Quick Adaptability

In an ever-changing digital landscape, adjusting quickly to changing trends, user priorities, and world events can be the cornerstone of effective social media management. Successful reactionary marketing involves monitoring current user discussions, staying on top of trending topics, and swiftly adapting your content strategy to resonate with the ongoing discourse.

Remember, the key to engagement lies not only in understanding your audience but in genuinely connecting with them. By integrating these socio-psychological cornerstones, you'll take significant strides towards mastering the art of social media management.

Chapter 8. Conquering Crisis: Damage Control in Digital Spaces

Not every day in the world of digital communications is a field of roses. The very online world into which you harness your budding business model is a dynamic environment where things can, and do, go wrong. Here, under our lens, you will find in-depth exploration of these "wrong" moments, what we like to call crises, and how to not only navigate them but also use them as fortification to build an even stronger digital presence.

8.1. When Crises Emerge

Crises, in the context of social media, often emerge when a piece of negative information spirals out of control, causing significant reputational damage. This could stem from a company mistake, a mishandled customer service issue, or even a well-meaning comment taken out of context. Regardless of origins, unchecked crises can lead to loss of customer trust, downturns in business, and a complex recovery process.

8.2. The Art of Crisis Identification

The first step in damage control is identifying that a crisis is occurring. Time is of the essence, as a crisis can erupt and spread like wildfire through the internet. An efficient social media management strategy includes monitoring tools to help detect possible crises, mainly through sentiment analysis, performed by software which provides real-time insights about the public opinion surrounding your brand. Keeping a keen eye on this sentiment trend can often nip a potential crisis in the bud.

8.3. Crafting a Response Plan

A crisis can overwhelm even the most seasoned social media manager. The key to effectively dealing with a crisis is preparation: creating a response plan. This should outline:

- Who will be notified when a crisis is detected?

- Who will be responsible for responding?

- How will responses be communicated internally and externally?

- Which channels will be used to communicate responses?

- A set of pre-approved messages addressing different types of crises.

8.4. Devising a Communication Strategy

Your communication strategy defines how, when, and where you communicate. During a crisis, it's crucial to maintain transparent, honest, and consistent communication with your audience. A well-handled response can help in regaining public trust, even if the crisis itself was damaging.

Your communication should:

- Be proactive: Address the situation head-on. Attempting to hide or ignore the situation may exacerbate it.

- Be empathetic: Show concern and understanding towards those impacted.

- Be responsible: Accept accountability, if applicable, without resorting to blame-shifting.

- Provide updates: Keep the public updated about what steps you're taking to resolve the situation.

8.5. Crisis Resolution and Learning from Mistakes

This final stage is arguably the most significant. Every crisis offers a wealth of insights to improve your future responses. Post-crisis analysis should include a deep investigation into the cause of the crisis and a comprehensive assessment of the response measures taken. This evaluation will help refine your crisis-response strategy, leading to more effective mitigation in the future.

In the digital realm, crises are nearly inevitable. However, with careful planning, quick responses, and valuable learning, even a crisis can serve as a milestone in the journey of mastering social media management, on your way to building a thriving digital venture.

Chapter 9. Monetizing Your Social Media Presence

In the bustling world of digital entrepreneurship, monetizing your social media presence is akin to striking gold. This endeavor blends creativity, strategy, and engagement, creating a space where measurable business value converges with social interaction. In this chapter, we will provide in-depth guidance on how to leverage your social media's latent potential, transforming it from a passive digital existence into a revenue-generating instrument.

9.1. Establishing a Strong Brand Identity

A robust brand identity is a fulcrum around which your social media's earning potential revolves. It's about carving out a unique space in the market, setting you apart from competitors and resonating deeply with your target audience. This doesn't just come from having a catchy logo or tagline; it must permeate everything you do.

To establish a consistent brand identity:

- Identify your unique selling proposition (USP);

- Develop a persuasive brand story;

- Design compelling visuals that reflect your brand;

- Generate content reliably;

- And maintain a consistent tone of voice.

Remember: Your brand isn't just what you say about yourself - it's what others say about you when you're not in the room.

9.2. Creating Engaging Content

Content remains king in the digital realm. Engaging content attracts, maintains interest, and ultimately converts audience members into paying customers. It encompasses a myriad of forms: blog posts, videos, images, infographics, podcasts, etc.

For successful content creation, consider:

- Regularly posting high-quality, relevant content;
- Utilizing a variety of formats to engage different audience segments;
- Incorporating compelling visual elements;
- Deploying user-generated content (UGC) to create a sense of community;
- And maintaining a consistent posting schedule.

Consider employing 'content calendars' to help organize and schedule your posts. These can help ensure you're providing value consistently and capturing those crucial moments of engagement.

9.3. Diversifying Revenue Streams

Social media presents a plethora of methods to generate income. These include:

- Sponsored Posts: Brands will pay to have their products or services featured in your posts;
- Affiliate Marketing: Promote third-party products, earning a commission for each sale made through your unique tracking link;
- Selling Products or Services: Whether physical or digital, social media can be an effective sales platform;

- Crowdfunding and Patronage: Platforms such as Patreon allow fans to financially support their favorite creators in return for exclusive content or rewards;

- Online Training and Consulting: Leverage your expertise to offer professional guidance or training.

Remember, diversification mitigates risk — if one stream dips, others might rise, ensuring a constant flow of income.

9.4. Harnessing the Power of Analytics

Social media platforms offer intricate analytics that track engagement metrics like shares, likes, and comments. Understanding these data enables you to adapt your strategies to maximize profitability. Key metrics include:

- Reach: The total number of people who see your content;

- Engagement: The interactions that people have with your content;

- Conversion: The percentage of people who take a desired action after interacting with your content;

- Customer Acquisition Cost (CAC): The total marketing cost to acquire one customer.

Engagement and high-quality content are bedfellows; understanding what resonates with your audience helps tailor your content strategy, optimizing for engagement and conversion.

9.5. Building Community and Fostering Engagement

Social media's power resides in its community-building potential, allowing people to connect and interact virtually irrespective of geographic location. Investments in relationship-building yield high returns in digital engagement currency.

To foster a lively virtual community:

- Make engagement a priority, responding quickly to comments, messages, and mentions;

- Show authenticity — let your brand's human side shine through, reacting genuinely and empathetically;

- Encourage user-generated content, boosting your brand's visibility, and leveraging social proof;

- Use relevant hashtags, making content easy to find and participate.

Turning followers into customers and promoters of your brand requires time, patience, and deliberate effort. However, once cracked, this formula mobilizes a fanbase, fuelling organic growth, and amplifying your profits.

By following these steps, you're well on your way to transforming your social media presence into a hustle that pays, opening up new dimensions of possibilities, profitability, and success. With a little creativity and strategic planning, your social media presence will bloom into a vibrant hub of connectivity, customer loyalty, and most importantly — revenue.

Chapter 10. Effective Use of Influencer Marketing

Effective influencer marketing is no magic trick; it's a strategic blend of creativity, analytics, and solid relationship-building. Let's delve deep into what it is and explore the tools of the trade, steps to formulate the most effective influencer strategies, measuring success, and the common pitfalls to avoid.

10.1. Understanding Influencer Marketing

Influencer marketing involves using influencers — social media personalities with high follower count and engagement rate — to drive your brand's message to a larger market. By tapping into an influencer's followers, brands can enjoy better reach and can often rapidly boost awareness and drive sales.

But knowing your influencers is the primary key. While Hollywood stars touting luxury watches may come to mind at first, influencers come in many shapes and sizes. There are macro influencers with over 1 million followers, like celebrities and top industry leaders. But don't underestimate their micro- (10k-100k followers) or even nano-influencer (less than 10k followers) counterparts! These influencers often have a more niche and engaged audience, and they can dominate influencer marketing strategies depending on your products and target market.

10.2. Crafting an Effective Influencer Strategy

A key influencer marketing strategy begins with clear goals. What do you want to accomplish — raising awareness, increasing traffic, gaining more followers or growing sales?

Once you're clear about your goals, find influencers who align with your brand values. Their followers should match your target audience. Use tools like BuzzSumo, Klear, and NinjaOutreach for influencer research.

Next, formulate your influencer proposal. Customization is key. Show that you admire the influencer's work and explain how your brand aligns with their values.

Finally, establish a budget for your campaign and ensure the compensation is fair. Money, products, services, or exposure could all form part of the compensation.

10.3. Measuring Success in Influencer Marketing

Remember those initial goals? Here's where they come into play. Influencers should deliver on those goals. Hence, insist on regular reports tracking metrics related to the goals. This could include views, likes, comments, shares, click-throughs to your website, and use of any campaign-associated promo codes.

Understand that flashy numbers aren't everything. High engagement rates can sometimes matter more than follower count. So, make sure your strategy is designed to achieve visible, but sustainable growth.

10.4. Avoiding Common Influencer Marketing Pitfalls

Influencer marketing isn't without pitfalls. One such potential hurdle is working with influencers who don't align with your brand. For instance, a collaboration between a vegan influencer and a meat-based snack company won't fly high.

Another critical mistake is neglecting to disclose sponsored posts, breaching FTC's Endorsement Guidelines and causing backlash.

Many brands also fail by not setting clear campaign guidelines. To prevent confusion, cover the frequency of posts, content style, hashtags to use, and any special instructions clearly.

10.5. Building Long-Term Relationships

Think long-term with your influencers. A long-term relationship can lead to authentic posts and greater audience trust. It's better to have a few influencers who thoroughly understand and love your brand than a sea of one-time influencers who may not deliver a strong message.

Great influencer marketing is about strategic planning, meticulous execution, and relationship building, coupled with a deep understanding of your audience. If done right, it has the potential to drive significant value to your brand and take your social media strategy leaps ahead. Now, harness these insights and embark on your own influencer marketing journey.

Chapter 11. Staying Ahead: Anticipating Digital Communication Trends

Getting ahead in the world of digital communication requires one to stay ahead of the curve strategically. This means anticipating future trends, understanding technological advancements, and being able to shift and adapt quickly and effectively. Identifying key trends early on can help your business stand out, and the potential gains from staying ahead can result in significant growth for your business.

11.1. Understanding the Importance of Anticipating Trends

Understanding the importance of anticipating trends in digital communication is crucial for success in social media management. By foreseeing these trends, you're able to plan and execute strategies that align with the future, instead of reacting to it. The digital communication landscape shifts quickly as new technologies are developed and as users' preferences evolve. This constant flux means that effective social media management requires up-to-date knowledge, flexibility, and foresight.

11.2. Analyzing Market Behavior

Predicting digital communication trends involves above all, understanding market behavior. Insights can be gleaned from several sources such as search engine analytics, social listening tools, and trend forecasting publications. You must keep your eyes and ears tuned into the digital industry, constantly seeking knowledge and learning to interpret signals that could indicate a changing trend.

Pay attention to audience behavior, their content preferences, the most used communication channels, most sounded topics, and analyses. These analytical readings allow you to anticipate trends, inform your content strategy, and run effective social media campaigns.

11.3. Utilizing Technology in Trend Forecasting

New technology is continuously revamping the digital landscape. Applications, platforms, and tools can help you spot patterns and trends. Analytics tools are your best bet for a methodical understanding of your present situation which can help predict future behavior. They can provide data about interaction levels, visitor demographics, popular content, and share statistics.

Artificial intelligence (AI) and machine learning are also becoming increasingly useful in trend forecasting. By analyzing vast amounts of data, these technologies can discover patterns and predict future trends with impressive accuracy.

11.4. Social Listening for Digital Communication Trends

Social listening is a valuable tool for anticipating digital communication trends. This process involves tracking your brand and competitors on social media to understand what's being said about your industry and identifying sentiments towards products, services, or concepts. Social listening offers a real-time insight into your consumers' thought processes, which can be pivotal in aligning the business strategy with the evolving conversation in your industry.

11.5. Evaluating and Adapting

The digital space is not static. Trends can change overnight, and what works today may not work tomorrow. Therefore, it's essential to have an evaluation strategy in place. Regularly assess your methods and don't shy away from evolving or entirely altering your strategies based on the insights gained. Adapting to change swiftly is often what sets successful businesses apart in the digital space.

11.6. Experimental Attitudes and Testing New Platforms

Embracing an experimental attitude is beneficial when it comes to identifying potential trends. Being one of the early participants on a new platform can offer a significant competitive advantage. Keep testing new tools, advertising methods, and platforms to identify what works best for your brand, and where your audience is most engaged.

11.7. Looking Into Future Trends

More than ever, the digital communication space is being revolutionized by a slew of innovations. As the spheres of virtual reality (VR) and augmented reality (AR) continue to expand, it's worth exploring these technological advancements as part of your future strategy. Similarly, understanding the growing influence of influencer marketing and user-generated content, and the ongoing transition from public to private spaces in social media, should figure into your strategic planning to stay ahead.

In conclusion, staying ahead in the digital communication space involves constant vigilance and adaptability. The landscape is regularly shifting, and as a social media professional, it's your responsibility to monitor, anticipate, and embrace these changes. By taking the time to understand, analyze, and apply these trends, you'll be well-positioned to keep your social media strategy relevant, exciting, and profitable.